MAKE IT SO!

DeVorss & Company, Publishers

Third Printing, 1990

ISBN: 0-87516-599-0
Library of Congress No.: 79-84946

DeVorss & Company, Publisher
P.O. Box 550
Marina del Rey, CA 90294

Printed in the United States of America

To all the children
who were,
who are,
and who will be —
and to the child
in us all.

Acknowledgements

To those who directly assisted us in the birth of this book, we give our sincere and heartfelt thanks.

Barbara Thomas, Frances Fowler, Richard Leo, Peggy Ray, Muriel Robbins, Muisya Sakovich, Karyn Martin, Keith Beery, Ken Thollaug.

We wish also to give our love and gratitude to all those loving friends who in some way contributed to us during this project.
Their love and support added immeasurably to our lives, better enabling us to Make It So!

MAKE IT SO!

Story and
Production Supervisor . . . . Betts Richter

Drawings,
Book Design and Production . . . . Alice Jacobsen

Special Editing. . . . . Frances Fowler

Part 1

You can **make it so** with affirmations.

Affirmations are special sayings that help your love-light * glow more brightly.

* That light of love within each of us.

1

They make good things
happen in your life.

2

Affirmations seem to be a
  magical way of
  making things happen
  in your life.

They are the words
    about your hopes and dreams
    that help you make them happen.

            They are special sayings
                that help your love-light
                glow more brightly.

Affirmations are for
    making your wishes come true.

3

I like to say these special sayings
    or affirmations over and over
    to myself, or out loud,
    or to write them.

I CAN DO THINGS

Here are some true sayings
about you and me:

I am lovable and capable.
(Capable means I can do
many things)

Something good is
happening today.

When I first said affirmations,
I felt silly.
I didn't know it's all right
to say such nice things, like:
"I am lovable, and
I am capable of many things."

Here are some more affirmations:

I am skating better every day.
I am running super fast.
I remember everything I need
    and want to remember.

I am drawing pictures I like.
Learning is easy for me.
I listen and
    I understand.

6

I am gentle and strong.
I am kind and caring.

My friends and I enjoy
being together.

7

Affirmations work because
     deep within each person is the
          kind,
               loving,
                    caring,
                         giving,
                              knowing,
                                   capable, and divine-self
                                   waiting to be discovered,
                                   and to give us the good we want.

8

We are all part of the Universe;

and the Universe is a part of us.

Each morning when I awake,
I remember the love-light
    inside myself.
I imagine it growing stronger and bigger
    until I am filled with light.
I imagine it growing still bigger
    until I am encircled by its beautiful glow.

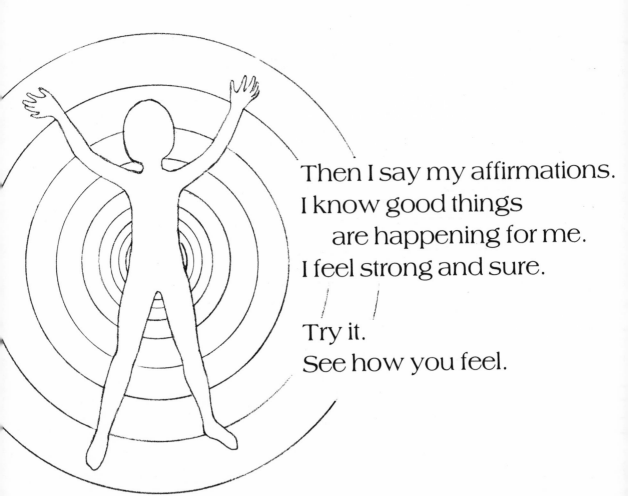

Then I say my affirmations.
I know good things
    are happening for me.
I feel strong and sure.

Try it.
See how you feel.

Sometimes I look at myself
in the mirror,
as I say my affirmations.

Sometimes I feel like
shouting them.

very special — smart — loving
kind — wonderful — strong
nique — happy — the champ
st friend — full of energy positive —
ce — healthy — capable
super
very special — great
a winner

Other times
    I want to say them to myself.

13

I say them at night
just before I fall asleep,

and I say them in the morning
when I awake.

Seeing myself doing
what I want to do
helps it to happen.

My wheels are fast and safe.

I make the goal
I aim for.

Jumping rope is easy for me.

Then I practice with confidence
and soon I am doing it!

When there's something
   I want to do,
   I think of my love-light and
   I make up my affirmation.

I say it over and over again,
   feeling sure it will happen.

I close my eyes and imagine myself
doing something well,
and being very pleased with myself.

I notice how I feel.

I feel warm inside and happy.

When I act as if I were
friendly,
loving, or
smart,

I find that I am.

20

GRAPE SODA
FEAST OF THE EPIPHANY (BALTIMORE)
PRETTY BIRD

GO BAR
WED, FEBRUARY 1

GRAPE SODA
FEAST OF THE EPIPHANY(BALTIMORE)
PRETTY BIRD

GO BAR
WED, FEBRUARY 1

I am loving.

I am helpful.

I am cheerful.

I practice being the way
I want to be.

You can, too!

Practice is very important
    if you want to hit a baseball well,
    read well,
    run fast,
    or be happy.

That something special within you
	already is all the good things
	you want to be.

When you act as if this is so,
	your best self is set free.

Then you can
	make it so.

Part 2

Sometimes I wish people would be nicer to me.

I wish I could change them.

But I have found that I can only change myself.

I know each person has a love-light inside,
    even though I don't always see it.

    So I say — "Now I see my friend's love-light.
        It's glowing brighter."
    Or I say — "I am finding ways to work and
        play with my friends."

I imagine having fun with them.

And guess what?!   It all comes true!

Sometimes I think
    my parents or teachers
    are mean to me.

So I say —
    "My love-light glows so brightly
    they can feel it.
    They love me."

I imagine them being
    kind and loving
    toward me.

Sad feelings melt away.

Before long there are good
    feelings between us
    again.

And sometimes, there are things
I want to change
but it seems too hard, or
even impossible.

Then I say:
  "Just for today
   I am helping with a smile," or
  " today , I am nice to my friend," or
  " today , I am getting
   all my work done early."

When I used to think:
    I don't deserve so much good, or
    there isn't enough,
    I'm bad,
    poor me,
    I'm dumb, or
    I can't,

I helped to bring just that to myself,
and I didn't like it!

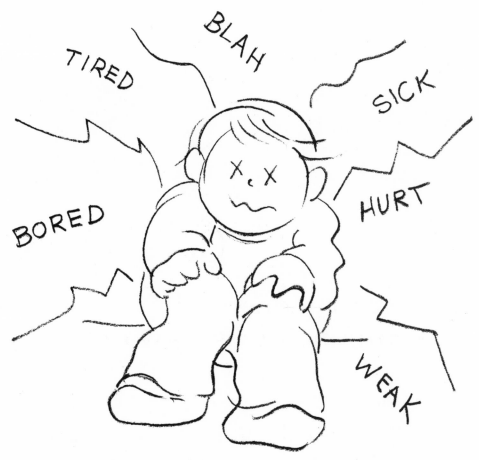

You mean we can
make bad things
happen, too?   Oh, oh! — Like what?

Well — for instance —
    I used to say,
  "I'm sick of this," or
  "I'm tired of that."

And often it seemed as if
    I really was sick, or
    I really was tired.

I'd say,
  "That's a pain in the neck,"
    and often my neck muscles would hurt.
I'd say,
  "I never win,"
    and I would lose the game.
I'd say,
  "I don't have anything to do,"
    and I would be bored.

So —

I've been wondering . . .
could most of my problems
be caused by me?

Part 3

We are always making affirmations
   and they work.
Some are useful
   and some are not.
They can make good things happen
   or they can make things happen
   that we don't want.
We don't always realize
   what we are saying, and that
   our words create our world.

They don't like me.

They do like me.

I can choose to like myself
  and others ;
  and when I like myself,
  other people treat me in a nicer way.

They want to play with me.
They want me for a friend.

It took me a long time to find out
that things can be different.

And now that I know,
I'm going to make
the kind of world around me
that I most want.

Let me see now —

I want to learn easily,
remember and
figure things out.

I want love, warmth, and caring.

I want to like myself and feel good.

I want to be joyful, pleased, and capable.

I want to be healthy, strong, and gentle.

I want enough of everything for myself,
and plenty to share.

So — I'm going to change my thinking
through my affirmations
and create the world I want!

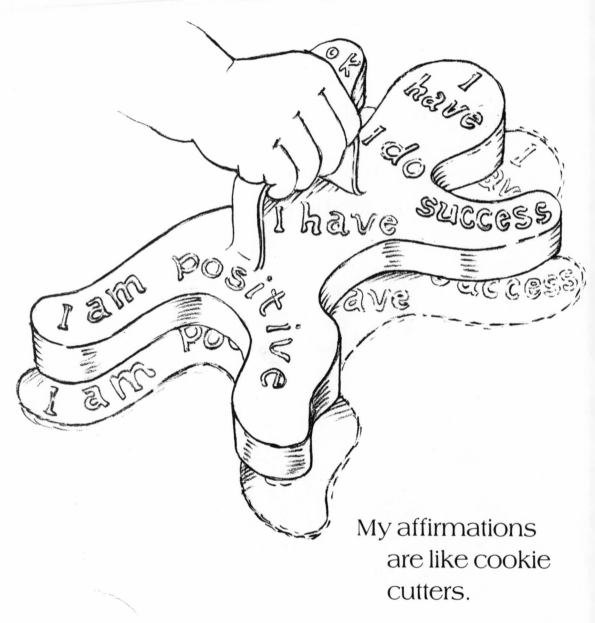

My affirmations
are like cookie
cutters.

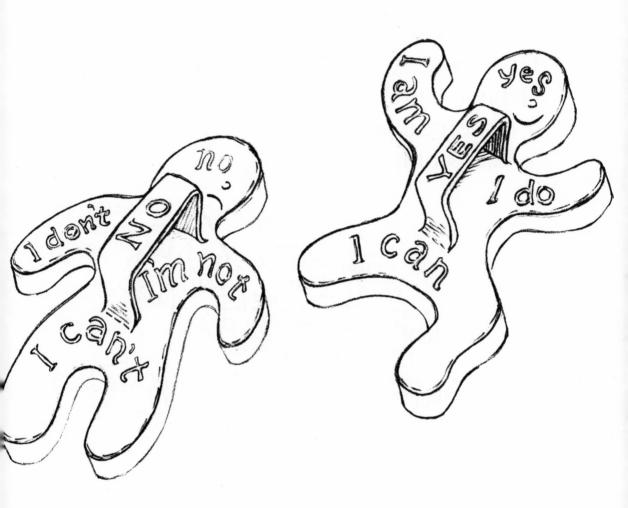

They shape the things that happen to me.

Here are my affirmations:

I am loving, warm, and kind.
I have love, warmth and kindness.
I learn easily,
    remember and
    figure things out.

My affirmations are like building blocks.

I am healthy, strong, and gentle.

I am capable.

I am joyful and happy.

I have enough of everything for myself,
   and plenty to share.

WOW! I like the way I feel!

I picture in my mind all my limits,
    troubles,
    barriers, or
    problems   dissolving,
                crumbling,
                blowing up, or
                disappearing.

I'm happy knowing that
    somewhere within each of us,
    is that part which already is
    all the good things
    we want to be.

We need only uncover
that special self.

Trust yourself!

Look for answers within.
Most often,
    the answers you hear inside,
    are the right ones for you.

Sometimes I need to remind myself
    by saying:

"I trust myself."
"My true self knows."
"I listen to my very highest self."

Usually I use an affirmation for several weeks,
or until I get a good feeling that

it really is so.

Then I change to a new one.

To uncover more of your highest self,
   just follow the directions in this book
   and . . .

Know that you deserve to have good
   come to you.

Know that there is enough good in the Universe
   for everyone.

Know that you are ready to have the good
   that is coming to you.

Let go of ideas
    which stop you from being
    all you can be.

Let go of all the things
    that keep you from
    letting good things happen.

Throw them away like paper airplanes.

HARD

Throw away:
  "It's too hard.
   I can't do it."

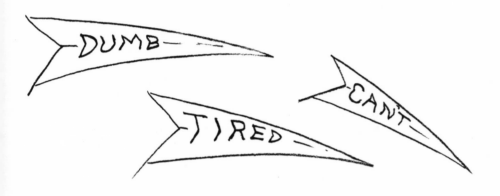

Don't say:
  "I'm not smart enough.
   I'm not strong enough.
   I'm not pretty enough,
     or handsome enough."

That's not true for me!
Or for you either!

Long ago, flying was only a dream.
That dream came true!
Do you have a dream you want to come true?

We are children of the Universe
   with abilities that are amazing,
   and the power to use them!

                  So let's do it!

Now,
  close your eyes,
  picture yourself feeling very good
  and succeeding.

Surround yourself with your love-light,
  and say:

  "I accept the good the Universe has for me!"

  "I am ready to make it happen!"

Make what happen?

  "Why — whatever I want to happen!"

So —
   now it's important
   to make room
   for what we do want
   by dropping
   blocks and barriers to

making it so!

51

You will think up affirmations
    that are just right for you,
    and good things will happen
    in your life
    more and more often.

The more good things that happen
    in your life, because of that
    something special within,
    the more your love-light grows,
    and the more happiness
    there is in your life.

Experience this all for yourself.

Feel the joy of discovering
that wonderful,

something special within you.

MAKE IT SO!

About the author:

Betts Richter, an educator, continues through this book to express her deep conviction that a better life can unfold for children if at an early age they are guided toward creating a positive, loving attitude of faith in themselves. Betts, a grandmother, lives and works in the Sonoma Valley, continuing in her search for a more creative, effective method of guiding children in their learning and growth.

About the artist:

Through the illustration, design and production of this book, the gift of an idea has been put into form. And truly, its creation parallels the message within it. Each of us has hidden talents and abilities waiting to be uncovered and recognized. Alice Jacobsen, also a grandmother, lives and works in the Sonoma Valley of the Moon, continuing in her creative expressions.

Betts Richter and Alice Jacobsen have also collaborated on SOMETHING SPECIAL WITHIN, an "awareness book" for children (published by DeVorss & Company).